FROM

Other Gift books in the series

To the most, most special Daughter
To the most, most special Mother
To the most, most special Granddaughter
To the most, most special Sister
To the most, most special Dad
Wishing you Happy Days

Edited by Helen Exley

First published in 2015 by Helen Exley® LONDON in Great Britain.
This edition published in 2023.
The illustrations by Juliette Clarke and the design, selection
and arrangement © Helen Exley Creative Ltd 2023.
Words by Pam Brown © Helen Exley Creative Ltd 2023.
The moral right of the author has been asserted.

ISBN: 978-1-84634-714-6

12 11 10 9 8 7 6 5 4 3 2 1

Helen Exley®
16 Chalk Hill, Watford, Herts.
WD19 4BG, UK.
www.helenexley.com

You can follow us on ![f] and ![Instagram]

To the
Most, most
special
Friend

ILLUSTRATIONS BY JULIETTE CLARKE
WORDS BY PAM BROWN

HELEN EXLEY®

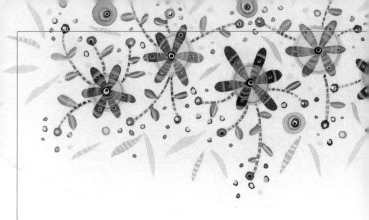

Friendship
is as commonplace
as bread
and breath.
And absolutely vital.

FRIEND

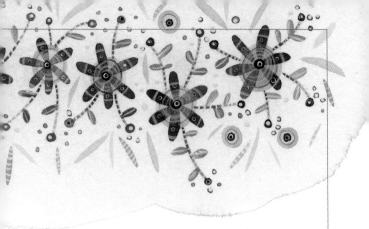

Real friendship
is akin to food and water,
air and sunlight.
Central to our lives.

SHIP

The world over...

The whole world over
friends escape
the monotonies,
the drudgeries,
of everyday existence.
Strength regained.
Sympathies exchanged.
Bitterness
turned to warmth.

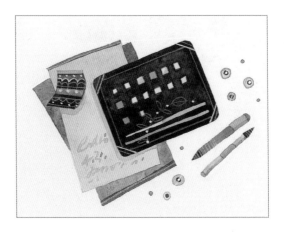

Friendships multiply

joys and divide griefs.

Friends know each other
better than anyone else.
We have shared
so many secrets.
So many sorrows.
So many joys.
So many fears.

The years have taught us
so much about each other
– our hopes, our fears,
our pleasures.
And how to share.

Friends
take each other
as they are.

The questions are never answered.
Only accepted.

A friend knows exactly how late you're
going to be, how strong or weak you are,
and makes adjustments.

Friends know lives are made of bits
and pieces and accept that some are
none too sound. Liable to crack or crumble.
Or lose their shine. But somehow love
and kindness bind it all together.
Friends know each other as they are
and love each other all the same.

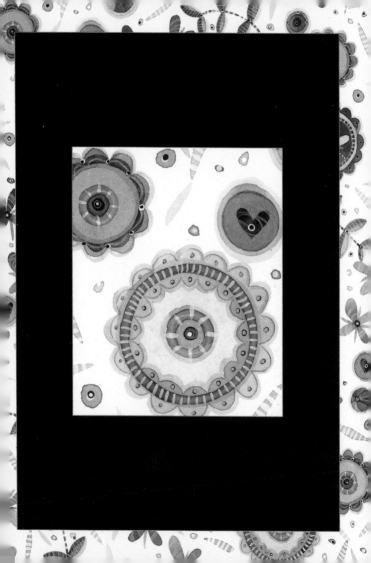

A good day
starts with
your friend's name
at the top
of your Inbox.

The phone.
Another interruption?
No, here is the voice of a friend.
And all's well.
And all is pleasure.
A lifting of the heart.

A friend is the bridge
into a wider world.
We see through their eyes
as well as through our own.
We listen more intently,
think more deeply,
explore a country
we had never known.
We need their care
and kindness –
and find delight in discovering
they need us too.

FUN!

Something funny has always
been funnier if you can turn to a friend
and you can laugh together.

Friendship adds an extra
brightness to any celebration,
an extra joy to each discovery.

Only with a friend
can one be really, truly
silly.

Friendships link
and loop and interweave
until they mesh the world.

We *feel more deeply,*
remember more clearly,
enjoy more if we have
a friend to share with.

People bond for protection,
for warmth, for help,
for company
against the unknown danger.
A sharing through which
the world survives.

Friendship
and kindness
make life
worth living,
even when love
lets us down.

A FRIEND
TELLS
THE TRUTH
GENTLY.

We who have friends
are wrapped around
in kindliness
and safe from the cold
immensity of space.

Friendship forces us
to be more considerate,
kind, forgiving,
thankful, grateful and
understanding
than we thought possible.

Friends mend
our lives...

Friends sew life together
with little stitches.
But sometimes are required
to embark upon a darn
or a turning sides to middle
or a massive piece of restoration.
Friends mend our lives
when they need repair.

However dark the days,
if we have a friend to turn to
we can find a way.

Time out!

A friend calls you up
on a sudden summer's day
and says "Drop everything…
we're going out
into the country
and finding ourselves lunch."

What's the fun
of an adventure
if you can't share it
with a friend?

You believe in me.

Thanks for backing me
when you
were absolutely sure
that I wasn't wrong.
And being understanding
when I was.

You believe in me
when no one else does.
You listen when you've heard
the tale before –
a hundred times before.
And you're there for me
when things go wrong.
You never say
I told you so,
but help me pick up the pieces –
and glue the bits together.

Thank you for sitting very still
and nodding in all the right places
when I told you some tale
of injustice and wrong-doing.
And making me a cup of tea
when I was done.

Thank you for Popping In to break the
monotony of the day – but
being wise enough to Pop Out again
if you saw I was hassled.

Thank you for popping in.
A head around the door.
"I'm going to the shops
– you need anything?"
Or
"Thought you'd like to know
the cat had kittens."
Or
"I baked too many.
Could you do
with half a dozen cup cakes?"
Dear special friend.

Who do I turn to
when no one else will do?
Always you.

You are my certainty.
When all else fails
you are there.
Patient and kind
and understanding.

constant support.

Dear friend.
Comforter. Rescuer.
Sharer of the ridiculous,
the hilarious, the daft.
Adviser. Helper. And supporter.
Standing beside me
when I needed courage.
Companion in delight.
What would I do without you?

You are necessary to my life.
For you, I snip cuttings from the papers.
And seek out books you need.
Watch videos that you have suggested.
Plant out more seedlings than I need.
Search the web
to solve your health problems.
Ring red around your anniversaries.
Enquire regarding remedies
for things that ail you.
Plan outings.
Worry if you do not eat.
Your life and mine are intertwined.
Despite all other claims
we need each other!

You have permitted me
to see the world
through different eyes,
hear things entirely new.

I've built an extension
to myself –
and it's you!
In you I find a wider world.

Dear friend.
Thank you for the first spring flowers.
And for fresh warm bread.

And postcards from far-off places.
And fashion tips for me.
And books you've loved.
Days by the sea
and walking in the snow.
Bus rides and small adventures.
Shared excitements. Sympathy.
And kindness always.

The potted plant on your doorstep
is from your friend!

The day was drifting by.
My hopes were raised.
My nerves were knotted
– but you called
and suddenly
there was focus.
And a smile.

A nothing day.
Nothing weather.
Nothing News.
No post.
And then – the telephone.
And there you are,
with wild stories
of stark mad Sat Navs,
and bursting pipes.
And see!
The sun is out
and all the world's to rights!

Without you...

Something awesome.
Or something appalling.
I reach for the phone.
I send a message.
I need a friend to share it.

Without you
I would still get about
but without being able
to share. The world
would be less bright,
less vivid,
less full of possibilities.

Thoughtful gifts

My home
is bright with plants
that you have
given me.
Your friendship
blossoming.

Friends carry
a list in their heads:
clothes sizes,
best-loved scents,
preferred shades,
best-loved flowers
and edible delights.
And so find you Little Treats.

I wish you laughter.
Spluttering laughter,
whooping laughter,
the helpless silent laughter
that sends you to the floor in tears.
Giggling laughter, heads together.
The shared laughter
in the dark of an auditorium.
The laughter that crowns success,
that springs from joy.
Kind laughter,
laughter that reaches out
and gathers others to itself.
And never mind who stares.

The comfort of a friend...
Our companion
in both joy and sorrow.
An arm about our shoulders.
A support.
A sharer of delight.

A good friend is a constancy.
Even at a distance
they are our kind companions.

Old friends can sit comfortably
in silence.
Staring at the fire.
Or watch T.V. together.
Sharing delight, ridicule or rage.
Friends review the world's events
– and offer sound advice
to one another.
Friends are easy with each other.
Content.
And happy.

A friend has the gift
of understanding silence.
When not to offer words
– to sit and be still and wait
until the moment they are needed.
When only they will do.

A friend understands
sleepless nights.
And leaking radiators.
And rising costs.
And pain.
And comes and has
a cup of coffee
and finds solutions.

A friend
persuades us
out of ourselves,
to understand
another life,
to share and grow
in empathy.

Thank you, Thank you

Thank you
for making me feel fun,
noticed, important.
What more
could I ask!

Thank you for allowing me into your life.
Sharing your fears and your excitements.
Your failures and your victories.
Your pleasures.
And so making me the richer.
Happier.
Your friend.

A friend is there.
Even out of sight and sound.
As present as the air,
the view,
the ticking of the clock.
A part of life.
A reassurance and a constancy.

At every key moment in our lives
our friends gasp and hold their breath
and cross their fingers.
But hang on.
Adjust.
And go on loving.

*You have always been there
when I needed you.
May I always be there for you too.*

Good friends
– for all time.

Your friendship has outlasted
fashions and enthusiasms.
Steady as the Pole Star.
My guide and good companion.

Your memories.
My memories.
Interlocked.
Times shared and full of dreams.
And here we sit
– remembering.

I am constantly at a loss
as to how, after all this time,
after all my idiocies and mistakes,
you should still be my friend.

Here we are, smiling in sunlight
– and as young as Spring.
A little less battered by life.
But still the selves we used to be and
not knowing what we know today.
Changed beyond believing
and yet
still friends,
and so unchanging.

Sharer
of anxieties.
Sharer
of silly jokes.
Sharer
of excitements.
Thank you
for everything.